Mess to Masterpiece

This collection of poetry
is dedicated to you;
to everyone constantly tired and trying.

Contents

Wounds of the World

Dainty, clean,

well kept and pristine.

Delicately dressed,

bright red,

soft and yet to be

worn down by

the roughness

of the world.

Jagged, beaten,

torn to pieces,

unpainted and tattered,

elegance pounded

onto the pavement

until calluses become

worn with exposure

as a piece of pride.

ADHD

I have what's called *Attention Deficit Hyperactivity*

Disorder,

but I didn't pay attention when they explained

that my brain rattles thoughts like rapid Morse code

and I don't know what the dots and dashes mean.

I can't remember names or my own birthday

because I'm tuned into the clattering thoughts.

Sometimes I wait for the rhythmic mess to make sense,

like trying to turn a math equation into poetic prose

and I'm really good at writing, but I almost failed

calculus.

Sometimes my own mind feels like a foreign formula.

My mother often wonders why

I never feel good enough

and it's because there's always a but.

Because the list of reasons why

previous partners have fallen in love with me

is the same list they give when they leave.

Being easily excited becomes *obnoxious.*

The spacey segment of my memory

translates to *you never listen.*

Every single symptom

equates to *I'm flawed.*

Some people say being neurodivergent

is a lot like having superpowers.

I guess because I can hear 17 sounds

at once and name them all without

missing the beat to my favorite song

that I memorized the third time I heard it.

Or the different accents I keep in my pocket

and subconsciously pull out

of my shirt sleeve like a magician.

But having an abnormally wired brain

is often more frustrating than fantasy.

I've had more therapists than relationships

and I can't seem to focus on myself

long enough for coping mechanisms

to make a difference.

But I would be so boring without the

chemical imbalances and zip-tied

connectors in my head.

I would be some sort of starched and

irrationally ironed version of myself.

Instead I'm worn and wrinkled,

still warm from the dryer,

stained blue and black

from being washed with new jeans

and an accidental pen in the pocket.

I don't want to be bleak and bleached

because my mental illnesses just make me

a little abstract and I've always loved art.

I'm still trying to get myself from

a mess to a masterpiece.

Graduation

I hated high school but

hated graduation more—

all of my female classmates

dolled in white dresses

to celebrate a fresh beginning

like a child does

the first snow of the season.

I was dawned in black

because I spent the past

six years planning my funeral

instead of my future,

writing apology notes

instead of thank-you cards.

My high school graduation

was just my visitation.

My classmates didn't know

they attended.

Coffee Stains

why god

do you test my belief

and put people through

death and grief

even when you're

buried deep in the earth

I'm suffocating from

your screaming words

memories of broken glass

from you tossing coffee pots

across the kitchen table

without a second thought

my cheeks are splotched and pink

stained from the pain

the tears welled in my eyes

seem to remain

Orchids

Unfamiliar faces,

hurt and shaking

over you.

I only recognized

a few.

The woman

with wild red hair

from the other side

of your old office

placed a single

purple-potted orchid

atop your

permanent

encasement.

She had tears

held in her eyes

when she suddenly

approached me,

grabbed on

tight like an

old friend

and whispered,

you

were always

the most special

to him.

Grass now envelops

the hole made

for your grave,

but nothing

has patched

the one inside

of me.

Years later and

I still place

a single potted

orchid atop

of your

permanent

placement.

Drowning

My sister has spent three years

constantly consumed

with afflictions filling her lungs,

but she calls it *coping.*

Everyone else calls it *alcoholism.*

I've been told you can't save

someone who doesn't want to be.

Maybe part of her enjoys

the suffocating self-harm.

Maybe I care deeper than

her darkness, but I can't

keep myself from loving

with every fiber of my being.

I just don't know how many more times

I can throw a life preserver,

have a hand to pull her out with

or the strength to do it,

because the moments

my sister realizes

she has been pulled out

instead of under,

she always dives back in.

They say *a drunk tongue tells no lies*

so why does my sister's only spin out

perfectly woven webs of barbed wire words?

She tells me that she loves me,

but only in a whisper when she's sober.

I choose to believe in only things softly spoken.

I can't count the number of times

someone has told me to *let her go,*

that *she'll learn on her own,*

but as children, we held hands

crossing hell instead of the road.

Maybe that's why we both

subconsciously search

for something that burns—

I study *Dante's Inferno*

and my sister always

tries to find flames

within leftover embers

that are not meant to be

reignited.

But they don't make

a manual for mental illness.

There is no formula to fix family.

All I have is compassion

and the same suit of trauma

we both keep hidden behind

hangers of self-loathing, locked

in our own skeleton closet.

I just wait, like a lifeguard

always on watch,

in case my sister has demons

that get too deep

because I know what it's like

to drown and the water

seems so much darker

when you're alone.

When I Speak

Words tend to tumble

out of my mouth like a game

of fifty-two pickup.

I can't always differentiate

the voice inside my head

and words I've actually said.

Somehow, you simply smile

and assure me *it's okay*

when I get frustrated about

the fluttering, messy deck

of sentences I toss out.

I always cross my t's,

but never dot my i's

because I'm convinced

it's a waste of my time.

I dodge and disregard

being told what to do.

If you asked me though,

I would carefully learn

to shuffle and bridge

all of my cards for you.

Love Is

A shot of adrenaline

any time her voice alters

because when it does,

she is different.

That's when you learn

love is when

her hands are a gun,

her mouth is full of bullets.

I am begging to pull the trigger

because I've already let her

cut my heart out and bleed me dry.

I'm nothing but a shell

of what I used to be

so I tell her, *pull the trigger.*

Because at least there would be

pieces of myself to put back together,

but instead she grabs a knife

and expects me to beg

for the life I've already given her.

She dangles the blade by my face

like a pendulum, counting

her patience and how many seconds

I am worth.

Love is sacrifice,

but not the kind I should be dismantled for.

Love is messy,

but shouldn't leave bloodstains.

Love is scary,

but not the same fear as

having panic attacks before breakfast.

Love is emotional,

but it shouldn't be followed by trauma.

Love is learning,

and I have learned that sometimes

everything is not enough,

but I am learning

I am still enough.

Summer Storm

You built up in the deepest of my veins

like blue brewing storm clouds.

Grazing the perimeter of your being

was more lethal than steak knives

shimmied into wall sockets,

but I never listened to my mother

when she said not to shower

in the midst of a summer storm.

I gaze upon the glittering city skyline

and find yearning in my bones

with regret in the deep of my throat.

Realizing how men are drawn to the warm glow

like moths to a flame, but no man

has ever loved me the same as city lights.

My mind is always a vast roaming sea

that returns like steady clockwork

to kiss the safety of the shore.

The surge you planted in my heartbeat

had a voltage never intended.

Vivid light crashed the space between us.

The sea of me stopped running

on ritual time. Instead of your name

falling from my mouth, it foamed

at the crests of splashing waves.

I catered your soul of soft clouds

until the midsummer storm came,

but I never listened to my mother

when she said not to shower

in the midst of a thunderstorm.

If you come looking for familiar waves,

I'll be in the porcelain bathtub

with the water still running in hopes

you'll return the lightning in my veins.

Without Withdrawals

Smothering eyes

and subtle breath;

you were

my cocaine.

I craved your presence,

but I've survived

the withdrawal

and now I'm better,

stronger, and

braver

without a thought

of you.

Insomnia

I can't sleep

so instead

I'll think of you.

The Steps to My Survival

It began simply

with basic motion

and transcended into

something great.

Falling for you

I was already

six feet in

and you decided

to cover

the grave.

Sometimes, I Hate the Snow

Winter is so cold,

bitter and barren.

Similar to those

who have left me.

How to Change the World

We all want to believe

we can change the world

but I think we are starting

to realize it won't happen with

our stainless steel straws

and plant-based proteins

because corporations

are corrupt and convince us

that we are the problem.

Unearth the Muse

Undoubtedly,

your fingers pat along to

the beat of anything that

makes you feel

you're still alive.

Searching for depth

in the shallow shore,

but all you find are

insecurities.

Keep digging for

something more.

The Sun Always Rises

White foam engulfs the sides of the ship.

Darkness surrounds the small craft

as the eeriness swallows you whole

with a barely vocal weep,

knowing nothing can be done

but to wait out the storm alone

in complete twisted mercy.

Your goal is to survive or

maybe just to see the sun

one more time.

Adrenaline Rush

We're all obsessed with a thrill,

anything to serve as a reminder

that our blood is still flowing

until it tumbles downhill.

Stop.

Find something to love

and save your soul

because I know about

the empty hole

where your heart should be.

Stop.

Before the metaphor

becomes medical

because something might

be missing but you won't

find it by trying to carve

out pieces of yourself.

Stop.

The future is out there

and I know because

I've seen it behind those eyes,

in between that smile.

It's in the sunrise,

the syllables of your name.

Stop.

Even if you can't seem

to find the lightswitch in

the darkness of your bedroom,

tomorrow will come

and will eventually bring you

a sliver of the sun to keep

going.

Dopamine & Whiskey

My blueberry tea

was never

strong enough for me

so at the kitchen sink

I would pour out half

and replace the hot beverage

with lukewarm jack

but now when I drink my tea

I don't reach for

burning brown liquor

to put in my

red floral mug

because I've

found myself

so goddamn

happy

No thanks to,

Josh F. — A real leader doesn't lie and degrade others. Good to hear that you're finally implementing suggestions I made over the past three years!

Jordan P. — I hope you've found a real sense of humor because suicide isn't a joke.

Laura T. — Looks like I'm not entirely incompetent, since I was able to write a book!

Actual thanks to,

Mama — I always appreciate the love and support you show me. Thank you for everything.

Hannah — You are my ride or die. I couldn't have gotten through everything without you.

Grandma — I always keep "those who are hardest to love, need it the most," in my mind.

Wilder — Thank you for telling me it was going to be okay and that you knew I could achieve big things.

Bobby L. — I am grateful for all of the lessons and little things you taught me. Every single day is a win.

Sammi — You are such a kind soul and will always be my truest friend.

Kasey C. — I never would have kept writing, but you inspired me to continue.

Colleen — I appreciate you more than you know for being helpful and supportive.

Avery — Thank you for always being you and encouraging me to do the same.